FAMILY SURVIVAL

by Jan Clark

Illustrated by Deborah Allwright

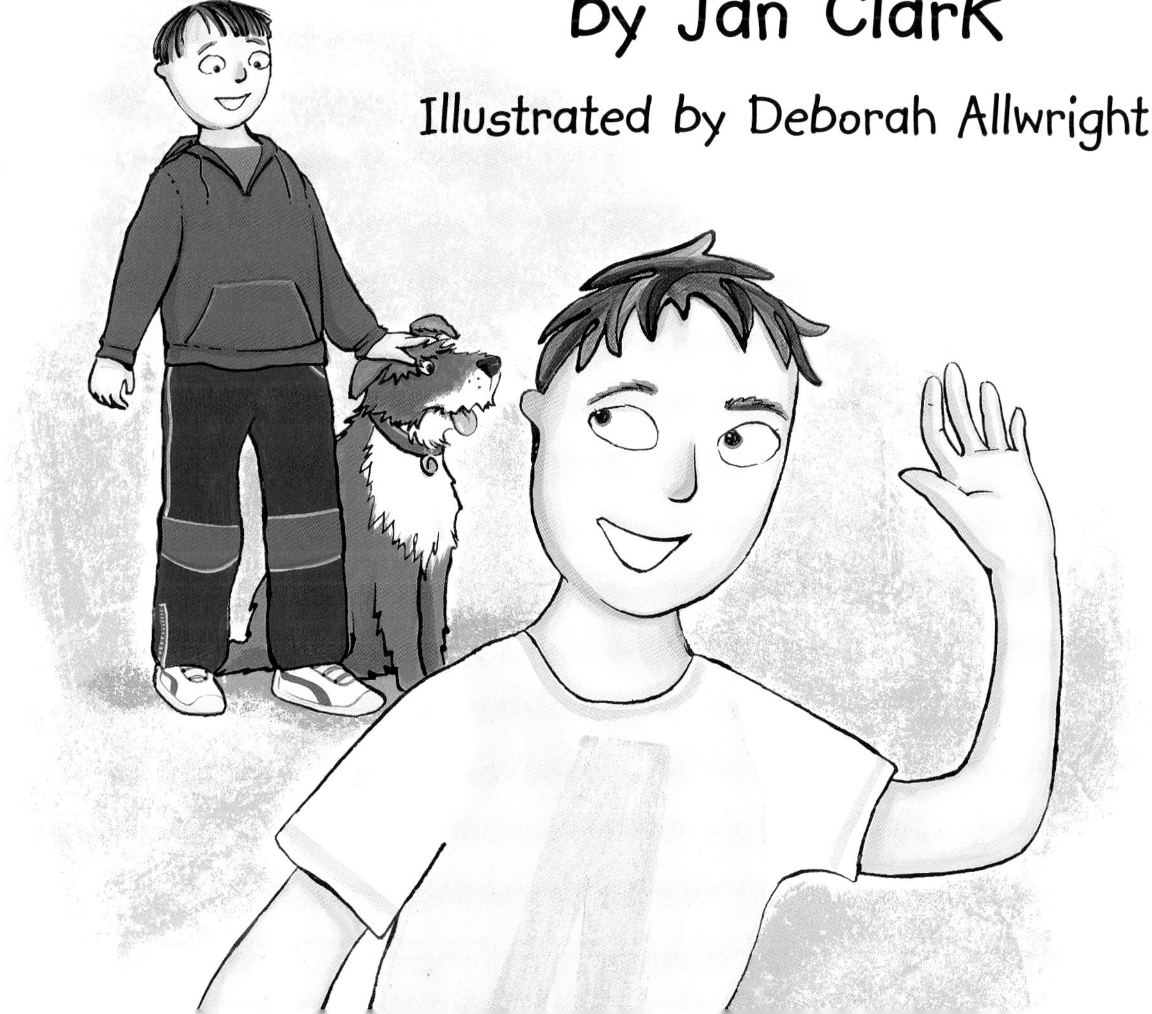

www.raintreepublishers.co.uk
Visit our website to find out more information about **Raintree** books.

To order:

 Phone 44 (0) 1865 888112

 Send a fax to 44 (0) 1865 314091

 Visit the Raintree bookshop at **www.raintreepublishers.co.uk** to browse our catalogue and order online.

First published in Great Britain by Raintree,
Halley Court, Jordan Hill, Oxford OX2 8EJ,
part of Harcourt Education.
Raintree is a registered trademark of Harcourt Education Ltd.

Raintree Editor: Kate Buckingham
Series Consultant: Dr Michele Elliott, Kidscape
Written by Jan Clark
Illustrated by Deborah Allwright
Packaged by ticktock Media Ltd.
Designed by Robert Walster, Big Blu Design
Edited and project managed by Penny Worms

Printed and bound in China, by South China Printing

ISBN 1 844 43419 2
08 07 06 05 04
10 9 8 7 6 5 4 3 2 1

British Library Cataloguing in Publication Data
Clark, Jan
Family Survival. – (Kids' Guides)
306.8'5
A full catalogue record for this book is available from the British Library.

For my grandchildren
Sharmani and Rowan (JC)

CONTENTS

INTRODUCTION

This book is about you and your family. Most families are made up of people related to each other who share a home. They look after each other, and the grown-ups work to provide the family with shelter, food, and clothes.

Families often enjoy activities together such as swimming, football and cycling. Some families have many people in them and some have a few. Can you see a family like yours in these pictures?

Growing up in a family can be lots of fun, especially when there is laughter and happy times. But **squabbles** and problems can arise, because it is hard to get on with everyone all the time. You may think you are the only one who sometimes feels upset, fed-up or frightened at home, but other children go through the same kind of things every day. This book will help you understand why families have problems sometimes, and show you ways to deal with them.

Let's talk about...

PARENTS

WHY DO I FEEL LIKE THIS?

It's normal to feel fed-up or angry if things have changed at home. Don't bottle up your feelings. Talk about them.

Parents are people who are mums and dads to children. Children need at least one grown-up to take care of them as they grow up from a baby into an adult. You may live with your real mum and dad or your parents may have adopted you. You may live with one parent because of **divorce**, or your other parent might have died. You may also have **stepparents**.

BUT WHY ME?

If things are not very happy at home or if you are arguing with one of your parents, just remember that in all families people do not always get on with one another all the time.

A parent's job is to guide you and help you to learn. They give you affection and praise when you do things right. They get cross when you don't.

I asked Dad and he says I CAN go to the disco!

Parents get cross when you...

- are naughty, demanding, shout and slam doors
- have been told 'No!' but go to the other parent who says 'Yes!', which then makes them argue
- are nasty to your brother or sister.

Parents are pleased when you...

- tidy your bedroom or look after your things
- don't grumble about feeding the rabbit
- are nice to your brother or sister.

LOOK AT IT ANOTHER WAY

Even though mums and dads love their children, it's hard work being a parent. If they are on their own, or have money worries, or lots of children to feed and get dressed in the morning, they can get cross even though you have done nothing wrong.

Let's talk about...

BROTHERS AND SISTERS

Brothers and sisters are **siblings** in a family with the same parents. Siblings may look similar, but they have their own likes and dislikes. They each need to feel special to their parents, that way they know they are loved.

I told you not to play with my computer. Do it again and I'll tell Dad.

Although most brothers and sisters love their siblings, they can annoy or get **jealous** of each other. They fight and compete when they are young but often become **loyal** and **supportive** as they get older.

BUT WHY ME?

Quarrels between siblings are a fact of life, because all children want to do different things at different ages. If you are an only child, you may wish you had a brother or sister and feel lonely at times.

WHY DO I FEEL LIKE THIS?

It's normal to feel angry or frightened if your brother or sister hurts you. But being angry one day and friends the next happens a lot. A grown-up should be told if frightened, angry feelings happen very often.

LOOK AT IT ANOTHER WAY

Brothers or sisters often think it's funny to tease or annoy each other. This is usually so they can get their own way or feel powerful. But it can cause very unhappy feelings, which you should talk about.

Rough-and-tumble games often begin in fun but end in someone getting hurt. **Spiteful** words can hurt just as much. Yet some brothers and sisters enjoy fighting, even when one is smaller than the other.

Here are some tips to stop things always ending in a fight.

- Don't lose your cool. Take a deep breath and count to ten.
- Tell your brother or sister to stop or walk away. Don't hit out.
- Try and remember that even though you may not want your sibling around now, you may become best friends one day.

Let's talk about...
STEPFAMILIES

Stepfamilies are made if a mum or dad remarries. You may stay with your absent parent a lot or you may not see him or her very much. Getting used to a **stepparent** and being part of a stepfamily can be an unsettling time. You may worry that your real parents won't love you as much when a stepparent becomes part of your life.

She always sides with her own kids.

BUT WHY ME?

If your parents split up, it's not your fault – it could happen to any child. It takes time to get used to being part of a stepfamily.

Your unhappy feelings are caused by the change. You will feel better when things get settled. You may even be happier because your parents are happier. If you feel caught in the middle of your parents, tell them it worries you and you just want to love them both.

It takes time to get used to being part of a stepfamily. You may find that you now have stepsisters or stepbrothers. You might have to share your bedroom. You might not like being told off by a stepparent. It's easy to get fed-up, argue, to hate them and wish they'd go away. But learning to live together as a family means...

I don't want to share my room.

- saying sorry for mistakes
- talking about feelings
- finding ways to help each other
- not blaming each other when things go wrong.

My mum's looked sad ever since my dad died. It's good to see her happy.

LOOK AT IT ANOTHER WAY

It's difficult for everyone, not just you. If you give it a chance, a stepparent could bring something special into your life, like helping to choose clothes, lending a hand with homework, or knowing lots about a favourite sport. A stepbrother or stepsister may turn into a great playmate.

True stories

MY BIG BROTHER

Hi, my name is Danny and I am eight years old. I live with my mum and dad, my older sister, Lucy, and my brother, Josh - he is twelve. Josh and I were at the same school until last term when he went to big school. Now I don't see so much of him, and when he is home, he won't play with me.

Do you want to play?
Going into town. Sorry.

He doesn't even take much notice of his dog, Raffles. Before, the three of us used to go to the park on Saturday mornings to play football - Raffles is a really great goalie!

Yesterday Danny told us he had been chosen for his school's football team – that means practice every Saturday morning. Mum and Dad are proud of him. I said 'Well done!' to Josh, but inside I don't feel happy. Saturdays won't be the same without him. It's not fair, even Raffles will miss him.

MY BIG BROTHER

Talking it through

It helps to talk to someone...

A PARENT

Danny told his Dad about being upset. Dad said he could understand why. He said Danny should be happy Josh is doing well and he needs to find someone else to play with.

A BROTHER

Danny told Josh it wasn't fair on Raffles – he would still need his exercise. Josh said sorry, but this was his big chance. He asked Danny to play with Raffles on Saturdays and promised to play with both of them at other times.

A COUSIN

Danny's cousin, Paul, said that the same had happened to him when his brother joined a team. Paul felt left out and really missed his brother. But he's now the star of his own school team, and his brother is really proud of him!

FORWARD STEPS

- **TALK**

  Don't keep your feelings bottled up.

- **CHANGE CAN BE GOOD**

  It might mean new friends and more choices.

I took Dad's advice and talked to a new boy in our class who is mad about football. His name is Alex. He and his family have just moved into a house in our street. I like him a lot. He says I can come round any time.

Mum and I went to Alex's the next day. Alex hasn't got any brothers or sisters, but he has got a dog called Floss. They came over on Saturday, and we went to the park with Raffles. Both dogs chased around in the kick-about. Raffles is a better goalie than Floss, she jumps higher to catch the ball. It was so much fun! When Josh came home from practice, he joined us too – it was great.

And now I'm looking forward to next Saturday...

True stories

MY PARENTS SPLIT UP

Hi, I'm Kimberley. I'm seven years old and I live with my mum and my little sister Susie. Dad did live with us, but he and Mum had really bad arguments. We couldn't get away from their shouting. And then one day Dad left. Mum cried and said he was never coming back to live with us. They were going to get a **divorce**.

Maybe it's my fault. I shouldn't have made Dad cross.

To make matters worse, Mum said we would have to move to a smaller house or a flat. I might have to change schools. I'm worried about my rabbit. Mum got cross with me when I mentioned him.

I don't want to move if I can't take Snowy.
Your rabbit is the least of my problems!

It's so **confusing**. Dad has gone, but Mum says he still loves me. I want him to come back and for things to be normal again – even with the shouting.

MY PARENTS SPLIT UP

Talking it through

It helps to talk to someone...

A FRIEND

Anna offered to look after Snowy if Kimberley was unable to keep him. She could see him whenever she wanted. Anna suggested that Kimberley come round for tea – her mum was good to talk to, if Kimberley wanted to.

A GRANDPARENT

Kimberley's grandma suggested that they help her mum together. Kimberley can help with Susie, and Grandma would help Mum try to find a new home near Kimberley's school, so she doesn't have to move.

A TEACHER

Kimberley spoke to her form teacher who said she was very sorry to hear the news. She suggested she talk about it in Circle Time the next day. Some of her classmates had been through the same thing.

FORWARD STEPS

- **IT'S NOT YOUR FAULT**
  Your parents may not be able to live with each other any more, but they still love you.
- **SHARE YOUR PROBLEMS**
  It can make you feel much better – and you might get some good advice too!

At my school, we have Circle Time every Monday morning. We sit in a circle on the floor with our teacher who asks if we have any problems.

I told my class what had happened, and noticed three others looking sad. One girl said she hadn't seen her dad for ages, but now she sees him more often because he's got a flat. Another said it was awful at first, but her parents get on okay now. One boy said he wished he saw his mum, she had rung him only twice since leaving home.

Everyone agreed it was sad when mums and dads split up but that what happened afterwards was different for everyone. I felt much better having shared it at Circle Time.

We did move into a flat but I didn't have to change schools. Snowy is happy in his new home with Anna. I miss him and I miss my dad, but I do get to see them a lot.

True stories

THE NEW BABY

Hi, I'm Jade. I live with my mum and my stepdad, Dave. I was so excited when Mum and Dave told me they were expecting a *baby* – I would have someone to play with! I helped Mum choose the cot and we put it in my *bedroom*, with my favourite teddy *bear*. I hoped I would have a sister called Barbie.

Then Mum told me it was twins, so I had to have another cot in my room and give away another teddy *bear*.

Why did she have to have them? Why weren't they happy with just me?
They are going to be so lucky to have a sister like you.

The trouble started after the twins, Rosie and Harry, were born. Everyone cooed with delight at them and joked about 'double trouble' but none of them knows what that really means. I DO! They wake me up at night, hardly ever sleep, and they smell. Worse still, Mum is always tired; we never do anything together like we did before.

Why can't she send the babies back, then things would get back to normal?

Talking it through

It helps to talk to someone...

A PARENT

Jade told Dave how fed-up she was. He said he knew it was hard for her, but it would be easier as the twins got older, then she would be able to play with them.

A GRANDPARENT

Jade talked to Nan who understood how much Jade was missing her mum. She suggested that Jade could help at feed times. Nan said that she would come and look after the twins so Jade and her mum could do something together.

A FRIEND

Jade told her friend, Jackie, who said she was so lucky to have a brother and sister. She said babies were so cute, and asked if she could come and see them.

FORWARD STEPS

- **BE PATIENT**
  You will have fun times again very soon!

- **THINK OF OTHERS**
  Try to think about how other people are feeling too – maybe you can be more helpful.

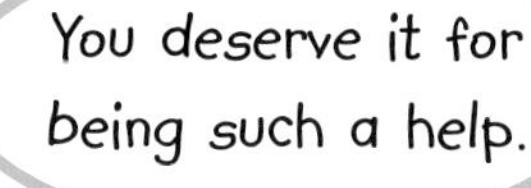

You deserve it for being such a help.

Thanks, Mum!

I took Nan's advice and help mum at feed times. The twins have been given lots of lovely clothes, so I put them in the chest-of-drawers. Mum says it is really helpful knowing she can **rely** on me.

One morning, I realized the twins had not woken me up. They had slept all night!

The next Saturday, Dave went off to play cricket with his team, and Nan and Grandad took care of Harry and Rosie. So I had Mum all to myself. We went shopping and she bought me a new ballet outfit, and we had an ice cream in the park. When we got home, everyone was asleep - Grandad was snoring!

I will look forward to teaching Rosie ballet when she's old enough. She can have my outfit when I've grown out of it.

True stories

MY NEW FAMILY

Hi, my name is Sarah. I'm eight years old and I live with my Dad, my stepmum, Julie, and her three children – Annie, who is thirteen, Jonathan, who is twelve, and Kate, who is the same age as me. Mum **divorced** Dad. I stay with her and her boyfriend every other weekend. Dad and I were on our own until he met Julie.

I like Julie but she is quite **strict**. Mum lets me stay up until 9 p.m. but Julie says I should be in bed by 7.30, like Kate. That means I don't see my Dad because he isn't back from work by then.

I don't want to go to bed yet.

The others are okay too, but Annie thinks she is so grown-up, showing-off, trying on Julie's shoes and make-up. The worst thing though is that Dad and I used to go out cycling together, but now Jonathan always comes. And he rides ahead with Dad, and I'm left behind. It's not fair, I didn't ask them to come and live with me.

Talking it through

It helps to talk to someone...

A PARENT

Sarah talked to her dad. He said Julie is in charge when he is not at home, but he will talk to her about bedtime. He said he wished he could get home earlier. He misses her too when he doesn't see her.

A STEPBROTHER

Sarah talked to Jonathan about cycling ahead with her dad. He said that he didn't realize she minded. He enjoyed going riding with both of them, and now he will ride behind sometimes.

A CLASSMATE

Sarah talked to Lorna, who has a stepfather. Lorna says it was horrible at first having to live with him and his three boys when she didn't even know them. Now it was okay. She said she would love to have a sister like Annie.

FORWARD STEPS

- **GIVE IT TIME**
  You don't have to love everyone in your new family, but in time you may end up liking them.

- **BE HONEST**
  People don't know how you feel unless you tell them.

Dad and Julie had a chat, and agreed I could stay up two nights a week until he came home from work. We have a cuddle, and sometimes he reads me a story. I have promised to go to bed at the same time as Kate for the other three nights.

I thought about what Lorna said and tried to spend more time with Annie. We tried on some of Julie's make-up together. We giggled so much!

Julie is not so strict now. And Jonathan showed me and Kate how to mend punctures on our bikes and fix the chain if it falls off. Now we have all got bikes and go out on bike rides together. It's so cool!

Quiz

WHAT WOULD YOU DO?

1. What would you do if, like Kimberley, you were moving house? Your Mum is worried about how you will cope and keeps asking how you feel.

a) Say you're fine (even if you're not) – you don't want to worry her more.
b) Get cross.
c) Complain to friends.
d) Tell her what you're really feeling.

2. What would you do if, like Sarah, your stepmum was stricter than your mum and you didn't like doing what she said?

a) Storm off and sulk.
b) Yell, 'You're not my mum, you can't tell me what to do!'
c) Talk to your dad about it.
d) Cry yourself to sleep.

3. What would you do if, like Danny, you were sad that your brother could no longer play with you?

a) Pretend it doesn't matter.
b) Secretly wish he'll get kicked out of the team.
c) Tell him you're proud of him but you hope he can play with you sometimes.
d) Be cross and not talk to him.

4. What would you do if, like Jade, you were upset by the arrival of a baby in your family?

a) Say you're happy (even if you're not).
b) Start being naughty so that they have to notice you.
c) Be cross with the baby.
d) Talk to a grown-up about your angry feelings.

Answers

1.d) Putting a worried parent's feelings before your own won't help. A parent will be reassured if you talk about what change really means to you.

2.c) Crying helps to let out the sad feelings you have, but doesn't change things. Shouting just makes other people cross with you. Instead, talk about your unhappy feelings as this can make things better.

3.c) Ignoring your feelings won't make you feel better. Ignoring your brother will make you feel worse! But if you say good things you will make your brother happy and you'll be praised when you do well.

4.d) Competing for attention with a baby won't take away your angry feelings. Tell a grown-up about how you feel, and they'll help you find ways to feel better.

Glossary

confusing

when something is hard to understand or jumbled up

divorce

married people who end their marriage obtain a divorce from a judge at court

jealous

the feeling of wanting to be like someone else because the other person is better in some way

loyal

believe the best of someone even if they are unkind

patient

remain calm in difficult situations

quarrels

arguments or disagreements

rely

trust someone will do what they promised

siblings

brothers and sisters of the same family

spiteful

people who are spiteful behave in a deliberately hurtful way

squabbles

small rows or disagreements

stepparent

parent who is not the natural one by birth, but one by remarriage

strict

imposing a fixed set of rules regardless of peoples' feelings

supportive

when problems are heard with attention, or there is active encouragement of an activity

Find out more

USEFUL BOOKS

Boundless Grace by Mary Hoffman

Grace is invited to visit her dad and his new family in Africa.

My Family's Changing: A First Look at Family Break-Up by Pat Thomas

A serious picture book about divorce.

Someone I like. Poems About People compiled by Judith Nicholls

A book of poems about our feelings towards our families and friends.

The Suitcase Kid by Jacqueline Wilson

A superb book for older readers about a girl going through her parents' divorce.

The Visitors Who Came to Stay by Annalena McAffee

A young girl's world is turned upside down when dad's friend and young son come to stay.

Two of Everything by Babette Cole

A story for younger children about two children whose parents bicker and argue.

USEFUL WEBSITES

www.itsnotyourfault.org

For those children worried about their parents splitting up.

www.kidshealth.org

Information for parents and children on feelings and how to deal with them.

www.kidshelp.com.au

General helpline for kids.

USEFUL CONTACTS

Childline
Freepost 1111, London N1 0BR
Helpline: 0800 1111
www.childline.org.uk

For those children who need to talk to someone outside of their families.

Kidscape
2 Grosvenor Gardens, London, SW1W 0DH
Helpline: 08451 205204
www.kidscape.org.uk

Helps children being bullied or hurt by others.

Index